"Accidentally Brave"

Pauline Savelberg

BookLeaf Publishing

India | USA | UK

Presentation by *BookLeaf Publishing*

Web: www.bookleafpub.com

E-mail: info@bookleafpub.com

ISBN: 9789358738476

First edition 2023

To my loving family - Paul, my husband; my sons, Matthew, David, James, and Luke; my daughter, Cassandrah; and my mother, who gave me my first poetry book - thank you for your unwavering support, encouragement, and belief in me. You have been my rock and my inspiration. Thank you for always standing by my side and for being the reason I never stopped dreaming. Thank you for always encouraging me. This book is dedicated to all of you.

ACKNOWLEDGEMENT

Without God's presence in my life, I would not be here today at the age of 62, writing poetry.

I am eternally grateful to my parents, who have not only given me life but also instilled in me the values of generosity towards others and the ability to appreciate the blessings in my life. Their unwavering love, sacrifice, and belief in my dreams have shaped me into the poet I am today. Every word I pen is a tribute to their unwavering support.

To all those who have served as teachers in the school of life, I want to express my deepest gratitude. Whether the lessons were joyful or painful, each experience has been a stepping stone on my poetic journey. I am grateful for the wisdom and resilience that these moments have bestowed upon me.

But my appreciation doesn't end there. My heart overflows with love and appreciation for my beloved husband, Paul. His unwavering support in handling the practical aspects of my book, from typing to printing, cannot be measured. But it is his unwavering belief in my talent, his willingness to listen to my poems even when sleep beckons, that has truly been a source of inspiration and motivation. Without his constant encouragement and love, I would not have had the courage to share my poetry with the world.

And to my dear friends, Rebecca, Doreen and my Uncle Tony, your presence in my life has been a beacon of light. Your unwavering support, your willingness to listen to my poems with open hearts, and your constant cheering from the sidelines have kept my creative fire burning bright. Your love and friendship have enriched my journey as a poet in ways I cannot express.

To all of you who have played a part in my poetic journey, who have believed in me even when I doubted myself, I am forever grateful. This book is not just a collection of my words, but a testament to the love, support, and belief that have surrounded me. Thank you for being my pillars of strength and for always standing by my side.

With all my love and gratitude,
Pauline

PREFACE

Early in my life, I was thrust into a world of trauma and loss, and I became intimately familiar with the raw, unfiltered essence of human existence. As the eldest of 10 children, I shouldered responsibilities far beyond my years. At just 5 years old, my world was forever altered when my little baby sister fell ill, succumbing to a debilitating brain infection. She slipped into a coma that would last for 2 agonizing years, leaving her profoundly disabled. The weight of this early loss settled deep within my heart. Then, at the tender age of 10, my world was shattered once again when my 8-year-old brother went for a swim and never returned, a victim of the unforgiving waters. The path of my life seemed eternally marked by loss, trauma, and grief, a journey I couldn't yet fathom.

By age 13, I found myself sitting in the office of a child psychologist, struggling academically, labeled as 'slow' compared to my peers. Little did we know then that early trauma can cast long shadows on a child's development. My journey through education was marked by relentless perseverance; I would study until midnight, determined to overcome the hurdles placed before me.

Through these early trials, I came to intimately understand the meaning of resilience and hard work. Life, in its capriciousness, led me to discover a unique gift within myself - a beautiful singing voice. I embraced this talent wholeheartedly, embarking on singing lessons that would bring melodies and solace into my life.

My path has been one of struggle, a relentless uphill climb. But within these challenges, I stumbled upon poetry, or perhaps, poetry found me. Life, with all its complexities, has gifted me with moments to write about, to pour my heart into words that resonate with the human experience.

Despite the hardships, I am profoundly grateful for each trial and tribulation. They have carved a depth within me that I might never have known otherwise. Now, at the age of 62, my dream is simple yet profound: I hope that every person finds their unique reason, their purpose in this grand tapestry of existence.

I fervently wish for all individuals to look within and discover the luminous giant that resides within them, to embrace the courage to let their inner light shine unapologetically. And if anyone ever tries to fit you into a confining label, I implore you to honor your inner voice, the true compass of your soul.

Above all, I hope that every individual recognizes their innate worthiness of love and respect, and that, together, we can uplift and celebrate the human spirit."

"Still and Tall,"

She stood set apart, from the others around her.
Alone,
Her limbs and trunk were tall and strong,
Her nakedness breathtaking.
She bared her heart for all to see.
Her naked heart seen by those that cared to look.
She knew how beautiful she was.
She was comfortable in her own skin.
People just wanted to look in awe of her,
Making up stories of what might have been.
Why was some parts of her so dark?
Yet some parts so light.
Why was she still standing after all the storms
she must have endured?
She is not alone; she has many sisters,
All with their own stories.
Her name is ancient,
Her name is tree.
She has endured wind, rain, fire, and snow, but
still she stands in such elegance.
Oh tree, the stories of storms weathered you
must have deep inside of thee.
You add such joy to my life.
Your wisdom and ancient ways call me always
by name.

You whisper, "Come sit by me,
Sit by me,"
As my old ways soothe your soul.

"I let her have her way with me"

She quit her job, closed the blinds, a room in black,
Her heart broken, her soul shattered; in despair, I found my path.

She came and consumed me, resistance futile,
I surrendered, letting her take control,
The only way to find an escape, to see the light,
To break free from the depths of this endless night.

She fascinated me, in her darkness I found hope,
For if I danced with her, I knew I'd break free from her grip's hold.

Confusion enveloped me, torn between love and pain,
Knowing her power to transform, like a butterfly from a cocoon's chain.

In that broken space, together we sat,
I yielded to her, no longer willing to combat,
No longer fighting against her relentless sway,
I embraced her hold, refusing to delay.

Tears flowed freely, in unexpected places they
fell,
Anger simmered within; her dominance I
couldn't crush.
Yet still, I succumbed to her power over me,
For in her embrace, I found solace and clarity.

Four years have passed, and I'm grateful we
crossed paths,
Grateful for the time spent in those shattered
aftermaths.
She changed me, ignited a song within my soul,
Unleashing a fire that made me whole.

Deep within, a newfound life surged and thrived,
Chains shattered, as I emerged, broken yet
revived,
No longer bound by the need to impress or
conform,
Embracing my brokenness, I found a love that
transformed.

So if she ever knocks on your door, my friend,
Welcome her with open arms, let her in,
For she will guide you through your darkest
days,
And in the end, you'll emerge, grateful for her
ways.

Thank you, my beautiful friend, grief,
For leading me through despair to find relief,
In your embrace, I discovered strength and
growth,
Forever grateful, I sing my gratitude song."

"A woman bleeds.

A woman bleeds in many ways,
Not just the way Mother Nature intended.
The female heart bleeds from the cuts inflicted
by others,
A bleeding heart caused by the choices of others.
Like a whip has torn every part of her skin, she
bleeds.
There isn't a lot of time for her to lick her battle
scars from her losses on the field.
She gets up like a courageous soldier,
Ready to take the next punch to her gut,
For her heart to feel like it will explode inside
her chest.
Heavy heart,
Heart in pain,
Heart that feels like it will explode with all it
contains,
Heart broken,
Heart wide open.
The female heart is a miracle,
Try to break it and watch it repair,
Break it, watch it mend,
Love it and watch it expand.
Heart wide open,
Heart destroyed, still not broken,

Heart that loves after the war,
Heart that will break but stand again, stronger
than before."

"Your music haunts me .

"He stands tall in the heat of the sun

Sweat dripping off his golden skin.
His long shades of brown hair wet from the sun's
rays.
Dressed in Native American clothing, he shines
nearly as bright as the sun.
He slowly moves his flute to his lips.
A sound is formed.
I close my eyes.
I am transported to another time, another place.
This Beautiful Native American Indian is all she
imagined them to be.
His music is haunting.
Every part of her physical and spiritual body
reacts to his music.
Goosebumps on her skin.
Eyes closed.
Tears rolling down her face.
A smile forms on her lips.
She feels her closed eyes glistening.
Her hands form a praying position.
She is grateful.
Every part of her is now more alive than ever.

She thanks this Native American man she will
never meet.
But her heart is full of gratitude for the sound
that only he can make.
Tears still falling down her face.
Hands still in prayer.
A spirit transported back in time and space.
For the music this brother plays that puts her in a
state of Grace."

"Sacred Whispers of Uluru"

In the vast Australian Outback, a sacred place,
Uluru stands with elegance, commanding space.
Its stillness captures hearts, demands respect,
As red hues radiate, a mesmerizing effect.

A love ignited at first sight, an instant flame,
Uluru's beauty, a timeless acclaim.
In the warmth of its red glow, wisdom whispers,
Sunset and sunrise, moments that astound and
blisters.

For fifty million years, this beauty has thrived,
Drawing souls from afar, its allure derived.
Rare is the one who can claim such longevity,
Uluru, a testament to nature's divinity.

Every angle, a canvas of uniqueness grand,
A terra cotta orange, impossible to command.
The land it stands upon, revered and revered,
A place to stand back, to marvel and be steered.

Some have walked its path, but words will
suffice,
To converse with Uluru, to heed its advice.

As farewells are bid, it's not goodbye, but 'til
then,
To linger longer, to hear stories from times
when.

Uluru, a minimal flow of nature's grace,
In its presence, a sacred and tranquil space.
May the next encounter be filled with awe and
wonder,
As the stories of this ancient land continue to
thunder.

"Screw those voices in your head.

Voices in your head, yep, I get it,
But what if you could change the tape playing in
your head instead?
The voice says you're too old,
Whispers that your boat has sailed long ago.
Inner critic playing games,
Ego growing out of control.

"You're too fat,
You're too thin,
You're too young,
You're too old,
You're not in the in crowd."

Says who?

What if you were to say, "Fuck you, voices in
my head.
Today, I take the power back.
I put those voices there, it's time to change the
tape."

You're not too old, nor too thin,
Nor are you too fat, or too young.

Screw that song.

Remember, it's never too late to follow that
dream.
Never too late to swim in an icy stream or climb
those mountain tops.
Only you alone get to decide when you can and
cannot.

...

The moral of this long story goes like this:

Don't die with the song in you,
Don't die with your poems inside.
Enjoy your life, this one crazy ride.
Remember the child within you and what it was
they loved to do.
Take your power back from the voices in your
head,
Don't let them dictate your life instead.

Today, I play the part of a poet. At age 62, I am
publishing my first book.
Only now have I given myself permission to live
the dream I had, instead of the ones that were in
my head.

" Ego you are not my friend.

Ego, you are not my friend,
Why do you pretend?
The true friend is the voice of the child within.

Child within, forgive me so,
I hid you so deeply within my ribs, you could
not breathe.
Child within, forgive me so, I was the adult,
I should have known.

To trust you, and you alone.
Why did I make you suffer so?
Why did I not let you out to play?
My dearest child, please forgive me for my
deadliest sin, the sin of blocking your voice.

Child within, forgive me so, come play again, I
beg you so.
I neglected you for so long,
All you wanted was to sing your song.
Child within, I remember as I glimpsed that
smile on your face,
I remember how you smiled after losing your
race.

I remember how you played in the sun's warm
embrace,
I remember how you wanted to look wearing
Marcasite rings and dreadlocks and things.

The hippie dresses and the way-out clothes,
Young and free you wanted to be.
I look in the mirror at who I have become and
it's you I see.
"We got here," you whisper to me, my little
inner child,
"See, you became what you had forgotten."

"The Rebel.

I remember the day you whispered in my ear, "I
see you."
I see the rebel,
Every part of my body reacted to you.
I felt more alive in that moment than ever
before.

Oh my God, he saw me.
He saw the real me,
The rebel,
The risk-taker,
The singer,
The poet,
The artist,
The writer,
The broken me,
The me with chains wrapped around my neck,
getting tighter and tighter.

Maybe if he could see me,
The real me,
The rebel,
I played the part of the good girl, but he saw
beneath my many masks.
He unmasked me.

If he saw the real me,
The rebel, in such a short time that we had spent
together,
Just maybe,
Just maybe,
He will find the girl that had died inside of my
heart and head.

I sit here today, and as I reflect on the old me,
I see that I was asleep in my own life.
How I lost her, I do not know,
But I promise her, from today, it's okay to come
out and play.
It's okay to come out.
It's okay to be
The rebel, the writer,
The painter,
The singer,
The poet.
It's also okay to no longer play the roles of
yesterday.

So as I approach my golden years,
Bring out the mess.
Bring out the smile.
Bring out the wild.
Bring out the artist and the poet.
Bring out the outrageous clothes and colors,

And don't forget those freaky, in-your-face glasses frames,
Because this old girl is about to play.
This old girl is about to be wide awake until the end of her days.

"Forget me not .

Sit and be, set yourself free,
In a world that wants to see you all but
shackle-free.

Sit and be, for just a while, as you feel your
worries start to dissolve.

Sit and be, watch the trees blow in the breeze.
Sit and be, as the sun hits your knees.
Sit and be, as the breeze blows on your face.
Sit and be, in the sun's warm embrace.

"Sit with me," cries the child within,
As the voice of the inner child screams louder
and louder.
Sit with me, remember how you loved to play.
Sit with me, as we remember the joy when your
hand touched the canvas.

Sit with me, as we remember the sounds your
voice made when you sang.
Sit with me, as we dance our dance.
Sit with me, give us a chance.

"Sit with me," screamed the moon and the stars.

Sit with me, my inner child screamed...
remember how we told ghost stories at night.

Sit with me, but forget me not, as I need you to
be what you have forgotten.
Sit with me, hand in hand, as we create a more
meaningful plan.

As the woman remembered the child within,
She smiled and laughed as she sat in the sun.
She laughed and sang at the wonder of what
would become.

" I am humbled today."

"I am humbled today".

I am humbled today, as the Lord in His might
Took away my blindfold, restored my lost sight.
Once broken and lost, with my head held up high,
I rode on my white horse, a knight in the sky!

But inside, I was blind, feeling lost and alone,
No longer the knight on his horse, brightly shown.
Now I walk barefoot, my feet in the dirt,
Humbled and broken, but finding my worth.

The Lord's intervention, a divine guiding hand,
Leads me on a path to a place where I stand.
With each step I take, I'm no longer confined,
Humbled and flawed, but a better place I find.

Though the journey is tough, as I walk on this earth,
I find solace and peace in my humble rebirth.
The challenges I face, they may shake my core,
But I trust in the Lord, for He's with me evermore.

So I continue to walk, in faith and in grace,
Embracing my flaws, finding strength in this
space.
Humbled I am, as I learn and grow,
With the Lord by my side, His love I will show.

"Sisters of the Well: Embracing the Naughty and the Playful"

"Women of the well, you cast a spell.
'Spell', you say?
Yes, a spell to tell all sisters it's okay to be
naughty,
And to come out and play.

'Play', you say?
Yes, you heard me, unlock those chains around
your neck.
Get ready to dance and prance and play again.
Sister, listen to that gentle voice in the breeze,
calling you to come sit in the sun and show
those knees.

'Show those knees', you say?
Yes, those knees that have carried you through
your years, they deserve to party and to play
again.

I know your life has tired many of you, but that's
why it's urgent to listen to that voice in the
breeze.

Take some big deep breaths, one, two, three, and
follow the direction of the girl within. Teach her
to smile, and grin, and sing again.

Sisters of the well, I know firsthand how tiring it
can be day in, day out, forgetting to slow down
on one, two, three, and acknowledging that fun
little girl that lives within.

This is the story of a 60-year-old who forgot
how to play, and sing, and have fun in the sun,
Until one day, the 5-year-old girl in her heart
demanded attention, demanded a new start.

Life is not for the faint-hearted, as we girls
know.
So find other sisters to hold hands and grow.
Be naughty, come on, give it a go. Now, be open
to the voice within that tells you it's okay to play
again, to laugh and to sing.

The creator of our hearts wants to see us happy,
with hearts full of gladness.
Created in love is where we all began, so get out
those paint brushes, paint, laugh, and sing.
But most importantly, the creator of life wants
you to forgive all things and learn to be okay,
because you were moulded in love.

We sisters were taught to go out into the world
to give of your all until nothing remained.
This 60-year-old wants you to hear, she had to
learn the hard way:
You can't help the world with an empty cup.
You need divine intervention and a full cup of
love, and to do all those things that you really
love.

Sisters of the well, you are worthy of love, so
take a risk, go dance in the sun.
Find the little girl that once loved to have fun .

"Day at the Beach"

She rolls in with such elegance,
A white aura surrounds her.

But the music she makes is sacred... music
created at the beginning of time.

She owns her sacred space so elegantly,
She knows nothing around compares to her.

The way she lures you into her space is deeply
spiritual.
I love the way the sun smiles on you by day,
But by night, the moon reflects such wonder.

Your natural beauty attracts such joy,
As dogs, kids, and families come to play.

I wish I could take you home with me,
And wet my feet in your cool waters,
Soothe me with the sound that only you make,
Until I awake.

"Come on Sis!"

I am only just becoming me.
I hope you are becoming you.
As I approach 62, I am becoming me,
I hope you are becoming you.

It's not too late for that outrageous hat,
And really, does it matter if you gain a little fat?
It's not too late to write that book,
Nor is it too late to study that course,
Nor is it too late to run that race, to go off
course.

It's time to blow up that box you put yourself in,
It's time to smile and have a sheepish grin.
It's time to colour outside the lines,
It's time to scream those roars you have inside,
It's time to dance and thrive.

I heard it once said a lady, 93,
Was told her life was nearing its end.
She said to the doctor, "It can't end yet,
As I have yet to live, yet to begin."

Come on, sis,
Dance that dance,

Sing that song,
Make right your wrongs.

Come on, sis, jump in the cold ocean,
Feel the sun on your face.
Come on, sis, walk that lonely bush track,
Eat that chocolate, so what, that's that.

Come on, sis, listen to the wind,
She calls your name, hoping you will sing.
Smile at a stranger, who knows where it could
lead.

There is a canvas calling to you,
To go get dirty and bring out little you.
Sis, get out and live your one life,
As time is passing you by.

So sing your song,
And join life in its cosmic dance,
Let your hair down, come on, take the chance.

I don't want to get to 93 and regret,
That I had never honored me.
So as of today, this 62-year-old gal,
Will start to change the things she needs to.

Losing friends sucks, that's for sure,
But life goes on as one door closes,

Another opens to explore.

We humans don't like change, that's for sure,
But we must move on and explore.

So that she has a grin on her face, ear to ear,
And people will see that she is here.
Age has no limits, the only limits it has,
Are the ones set by you.

"My Mantra"

Take the good parts of yourself and love them
like no other.
The parts of you that you don't like, try harder.
I have a mantra: "Make me a better human
being."
Kinder, gentler, more loving, more forgiving,
Grant me endless amounts of generosity to
sprinkle wherever I go.
Let me shine like the sun, to not play small for
anyone.
To stand tall like a sunflower, reaching for the
sky.
Kinder than before, like a high jump jumper,
jumping towards the sky.
Gentler, I aim to be. This is my mantra, and I
love being me.
Aim high, stand tall.
Be strong like a lion, let them hear you roar.

"Empty Nester,"

"I am just a mum of five," was the thought in her
head.
One crisp winter's morning, she awoke and
discovered she could write.
It was said that creativity could be unlocked, like
a thief in the night, after facing adversity. So it is
said, whispered wisdom gently in her ear.

Her heart had been heavy of late, there had been
many losses for her to take.
Being a mum was the only purpose she could
see in her sight.
But as all things do, babies turn into adults and
leave home.
She crumbled in blackness onto her knees,
scared and alone.

"Who am I without my children?" she thought.
"No joy ahead," was her deepest fear.
"Empty nester," I think it's called,
But this label was not kind, not kind to her at all.

One by one, the birds left the nest.
The mother of five was sad for a while, but that
is not the end of this story being told.

She sat with her grief, as brave as a knight on his
white horse.
Healed and transformed of her despair,
She took out a pen and put it to paper.
Poem after poem did this brave mum write, and
kids' books too.
This mum of five now calls herself a poet, and
she is about to travel overseas.
So maybe being an empty nester is far more fun
than she thought.
Once you're over your empty nest blues,
I know deep in the pit of my gut,
You will open a new door,
The next stage,
And soar.

"Beyond the Labels:

My children's diagnosis, I hear them say,
Their thoughts and words, they freely convey.
But if I look within, I'll find much more,
Beyond the label they try to explore.

Emotions run deep, I feel with intensity,
Trips planned impulsively, leading to fatigue's
entity.
ADHD, they claim, but I smile in jest,
No label can confine the spirit I invest.

Bold glasses adorn, a statement of flair,
Bare feet, my preference, freedom in the air.
Pairing shoes with socks, a playful art,
ADHD, perhaps, but it's been there from the
start.

In my own skin, contentment resides,
Labels may come, but my trust abides.
So go ahead, give me a label if you must,
But this old girl knows herself, in her she'll trust.

"Dark Clouds and Sunflowers"

The storm clouds loomed near,
Closer than she had feared.
They raced, fierce and fast,
Lightning striking, trees harassed.

She sensed their approach,
Closing in with menacing reproach.
She tried to push them away,
But they chose chaos for this day.

Thought-stopping and deep breaths,
Failed to calm the storm's dark depths.
She knew they were meant for her,
Destined to disturb and to stir.

Above her hairline, they settled,
Black clouds, heavy and unkind settled.
For three days, they lingered low,
Testing her strength, her will to grow.

But after three days, she emerged,
Opening her door, letting light surge.
"Oh sun, my friend, welcome here,
Those black storms had me living in fear.

But now, with you by my side,
I sprinkle sunflowers, grins worldwide.
Dark clouds, you're a part of me,
But I choose how long you'll be.

Be grateful for your three-day stay,
For I embrace the sun's radiant array."

"The dance of Joy and Tears"

With a gigantic character, you stand,
Incomparable, unmatched in all the land.
Wherever you go, joy and happiness bloom,
In your presence, the world finds room.

Thoughts of you spark movements deep,
Within my being, emotions seep.
Awakening my heart and soul's fire,
With you, I'm filled with pure desire.

It's amusing how you bring both joy and tears,
Simultaneously, my emotions steer.
Tears flow swiftly down my face,
While joy abounds in your embrace.

Honestly, thinking of you stirs emotion,
I can't help but feel a deep devotion.
Thankful for the challenges we endure,
Together, we find strength and ensure.

Eternally in awe of your power over me,
You're one of the best things, you see.
Gratitude fills my heart, I must confess,
Thank you, my beautiful friend, for all the
happiness.

"Whispers in the Rain"

She was filled with excitement as she heard the
noise emanating from her backyard.

Drip, drip, drip; drops on the iron metal roof.
Oh, what a joyous sound it made.

She opened her door and her instincts were
correct;
It was an overcast rainy day.
Oh, excitement consumed this 62-year-old
woman's body, reminiscent of the pure joy felt
by a 7-year-old child.

She took a deep breath, inhaling the damp air.
She had so many plans for the day,
But if she truly listened, she could hear the soft
whispers of her body saying, "I am tired."

As the woman closed her door,
She took a few more deep breaths
And granted herself permission to simply exist
for the day.
She felt a surge of anticipation for the new
possibilities that the rain brought with it.
It was time for her to just be.

Time for her to express gratitude for this day,
Not to mention her garden silently singing
praises for the nourishment of the rain.

It was a moment to rest and attune to the inner
whispers yearning to be heard.
The woman closed her eyes and honored herself
and this perfect day.

"Embraced by Cairns: A Love Rekindled"

I feel like I'm going to burst from deep within,
After 28 years, you still stir me, my heart does spin.
Tears threaten to escape, like a rushing tide,
Oh, Cairns, you leave me weak, my knees can't hide.

That subtle breeze, a part of your alluring grace,
The swaying palm trees, hypnotic in their embrace.
How can I not feel like a child, filled with pure joy,
Ready to explode, like a playful, exuberant toy?

28 years ago, I fell for your climate so rare,
Your green landscape, stretching beyond compare.
But it's the swaying trees and the enchanting breeze,
That touch my soul the most, bringing me to my knees.

Thank you for reigniting the love I held for you,
I cherish being me, feeling emotions so true.

Cairns, you've shown me a world within your domain,
And for that, I am grateful, finding peace and gain.